The Classical Guitarist's Gig Book
Volume 2

Creative Transcriptions for Today's Guitarist

by

Mark Anthony Cruz

MEL BAY

WWW.MELBAY.COM

Index

Affettuoso (from Sonata for Flute, RV 48) – Vivaldi 18
All Creatures of Our God and King – Hymn 118
Allegro – Haydn 22
Allegro (from Concerto in D, RV 93) – Vivaldi 21
Alman – Johnson 11
Amazing Grace – Hymn 116
Andante (from Concerto for Two Mandolins, RV 532) – Vivaldi 38
Angels We Have Heard on High – Traditional French 108
Anitra's Dance (from Peer Gynt - Suite No. 1 Op. 46) – Grieg 48
Arrival of the Queen of Sheba, The - Handel 42
Ballo 'plus de tristesse ta maitresse' – Milano 14
Battle Hymn of the Republic – American Folk Song 26
Cello Suite No. 1 (BWV 1007) – Bach
- Allemande 62
- Courante 64
- Gigue 68
- Menuet I 66
- Menuet II 67
- Prelude 59
- Sarabande 66

Christ The Lord Has Risen Today – Hymn 126
Come Again – Dowland 12
Couplet (Combined studies from Sixty Short Reading Exercises, Studies and Pieces) – Cruz 16
Coventry Carol – English 14th Century 110
Divertimento – Cruz
- III. Air 101
- IV. Capricho 102
- I. Rondo 98
- II. Sonata 100

Fugue (BWV 1000) – Bach 74
Für Elise – Beethoven 56
God Rest Ye, Merry Gentlemen (Theme and Variations) – English Tune 105

God Save the Queen (Op. 6, No. 10) – Traditional ... 25
Guárdame las Vacas – Narváez ... 10
Hornpipe (No. 13 from Water Musik HWV 349) – Handel ... 40
In the Hall of the Mountain King (from Peer Gynt - Suite No. 1 Op. 46) – Grieg ... 46
Julia Florida – Barrios Mangoré ... 94
Kossler Prelude (from Prelude and Fugue in d Minor) – Cruz ... 54
Lascia Ch'io Pianga (Aria from Rinaldo) – Handel ... 20
Londonderry Air (Danny Boy) – Traditional Irish Melody ... 33
Malagueña – Cruz ... 84
Malagueña Fácil Tárrega ... 82
March of the Toys (from Babes in Toyland) – Herbert ... 113
Maria (Gavotte) – Tárrega ... 80
Military March No. 1 (from Pomp and Circumstance Military Marches, Op. 39) – Elgar ... 28
Minuetto and Trio (from Grande Sonata, Op. 25) – Sor ... 19
O Sacred Head Now Wounded (Matthew Passion) – Bach ... 96
Overture – Carulli ... 86
Pavan No. 1 – Milan ... 8
Pavan No. 3 – Milan ... 9
Polovtsian Dance (from Prince Igor) – Borodin ... 50
Prelude (BWV 999) – Bach ... 72
Rondo (Op. 2, No. 3) – Aguado ... 120
Sheep May Safely Graze (from Cantata BWV 208) – Bach ... 34
Sicilienne (Op. 78) – Fauré ... 52
Sleepers, Wake (from Cantata No. 140, BWV 645) – Bach ... 36
Sonata K. 334 – Scarlatti ... 69
Ständchen – Schubert ... 23
Star-Spangled Banner, The – Smith ... 24
Study No. 57 (from Sixty Short Reading Exercises, Studies and Pieces) – Cruz ... 17
Thaxted (excerpt from Jupiter from The Planets) – Holst ... 31
Trumpet Tune – Clarke ... 30
Vals (Op. 8, No. 4) – Barrios Mangoré ... 91
Water Is Wide, The – Scottish Folk Song ... 32
Wedding Day at Tröldhaugen (Op. 65, No. 6) – Grieg ... 29

Legend

Two types of barre notations have traditionally been used until recently. The use of the letter C (first letter of the Spanish word, Ceja, for barre) instructs the player to barre across all six strings with the left-hand index finger (Example 1). Example 2 instructs the player to barre only half the strings rather than all six. This may also imply a barre of four strings or perhaps less than three, depending on what the music implies.

Ex. 1: **CIII** Ex. 2: **ȻV**

The latter instruction, in many cases, can be unclear or ambiguous. Therefore, the modern barre notation system used in this source is designed to look less cluttered while providing more specificity.

The Roman numeral, alone, is used to imply a full bar across all six strings (Example 3 - barre all six strings).

The notation of barring a specific number of strings is indicated by the placement of a superscript number to the upper-right of the Roman numeral (Example 4 - barre four strings in m. 1 and five strings in m.2).

Ex. 3

Ex. 4

Hinge barres or partial barres are notated with an h. These instruct the player to either fret the first string with the base of the first finger (Example 5) or to play a set of lower strings with the whole first finger tip joint (Example 6). The music will imply one or the other.

Ex. 5

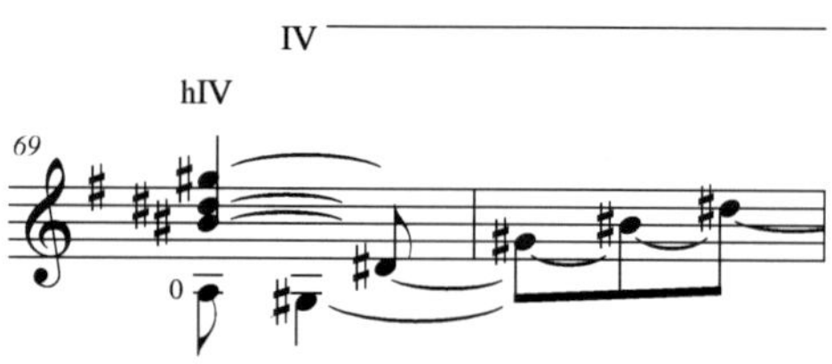

Ex. 6

Left-hand fingerings are represented by numbers: 1, 2, 3, 4

Circled numbers represent strings ⑥ through ①, six being the largest or lowest bass string. These are used to indicate that a note should be played on a specific string.

Ex. 7

Foreword

I have had the great pleasure of knowing Mark Cruz for many years as an accomplished performer, composer, teacher, and as a friend. He occupies a rather unique place in the American classical guitar profession, especially Texas and Oklahoma, as one of the most influential acoustic guitarists in the Southwest region for decades. I have had the honor of introducing a few of his guitar ensemble compositions in Austin as they were selected by Austin Classical Guitar from a competitive field of submissions. Whether ensemble or solo, his music is always joyful and evocative. He has a highly developed combination of creative skill and teaching experience that comes together in outstanding fashion in this assortment of musical selections.

Mark Cruz is a musician who has explored a breadth of artistic expression in a varied and creatively challenging way. This collection reflects that work across a huge range of musical style. Besides the obvious variety of mood and character represented here, the value to musicians and music students is also clear. When a professional solo guitarist provides music for a variety of events, there is an obvious need for collections such as this. In Cruz's compendium there is the rare combination of sacred and secular music that is both rewarding and accessible.

For education purposes, the selections were edited for technical ease and with expressive opportunity in mind. The arrangements for popular classics are a welcome addition to this collection that can supply a long term and enjoyable resource for developing both technique and repertoire. Teachers will find the music in this publication to be a wealth of pieces for student technical needs and diverse musical tastes.

Never one to be musically shy, Mark has proven his ability as an impressive improvisor, composer, arranger, and an astute interpreter of classical music genres. This collection of pieces embodies the skill and sensitivity acquired and refined through those creative outlets.

Dr. Michael Quantz,

UT System Regent's Outstanding Teaching Award recipient
NAfME All-National Honors Guitar Ensemble inaugural conductor

A Note from the Author

With the fruition of the first volume of *The Classical Guitarist's Gig Book* around the outbreak of the 2020 pandemic and the closing of the US economy, I realized that I would have an unusual amount of time on my hands. I decided to make it my goal to create a second volume consisting of sixty-three pieces (to match the first volume) within the boundaries of late March 2020 to the beginning of the 2020 fall semester which occurred in late August. I was able to accomplish that goal without a day to spare. Hence, I refer to Volume II as the "pandemic anthology."

Similar to the first, Volume II includes familiar classical works but differs with the addition of hymns, patriotic and Christmas selections. Many of these were absorbed from early projects that I revisited with the task of improving their development and structural content.

Admittedly, *Angels We Have Heard on High* is stylistically unbalanced. The reason for this is that it is presented in three versions: the first is traditional, simplified and condensed; the second is modern with chord substitutions and with the chorus offset by half a beat; and the third is traditional with mild chord substitutions, two short original interludes and the most developed and challenging to play of the three. Collectively, it is designed for not only length but also to provide the listener with musical diversity and surprises.

I have included two versions of *Malagueña.* The first is Francisco Tárrega's and the second is original. These can be performed separately or as one piece for a larger form and a continuous flow of changing musical content. Such a pairing would offer a unique performance experience of this familiar work.

Regarding creative transcriptions, the first in this volume is *Come Again* by John Dowland. I added an introduction and a closing section which I borrowed from one of Dowland's fantasies.

Such an adjustment might not qualify as something creative, but it does assert an idea not yet presented until now. The creative aspects in this rendition include the usual chord substitutions, scales and a variation on the theme followed by a coda.

Two traditional pieces, *The Water is Wide* and *Londonderry Air* (better known as *Danny Boy*), maintain their melodic integrity, but I present each in modern harmony (one more than the other). Other than the bulk of the hymns and Christmas tunes being emphatically composition-based, the remainder of the book is adaption-based with the exception of a few minor tweaks.

The original works, of course, provided me opportunities to explore greater compositional creativity. There are many represented within this compendium. My *Malagueña* might be considered a pastiche piece but nonetheless offers a refreshing angle. The four-movement *Divertimento* is influenced by Baroque and Classical styles. The themes for the last three movements were derived through thematic transformation from the theme of the first movement - the most obvious being the last movement which is an inversion of the first movement.

Movement I (Rondo)

Movement IV (Capricchio)

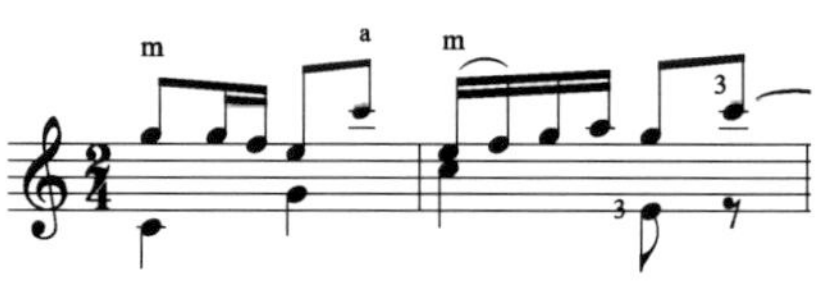

Finally, I composed *Kossler Prelude* around the beginning of the pandemic. Commissioned by Adam Kossler for his guitar duo, it is a solo guitar reduction from the first movement of the *Prelude and Fugue* for two guitars in d minor.

Just as is stated in Volume I, I do not claim that my choices in this anthology are better or definitive, but rather they are simply alternatives to other editions. Understanding that there are numerous ways to finger guitar music, the fingerings that I have chosen are specific to my technical ease but might not translate well for someone else; therefore, I encourage re-fingering if the performer is so inclined. If one should identify an absence of voices or slight changes within certain pieces, it is for the purpose of creating an idiomatic solution. Finally, the avoidance of string noise from shifting across the basses (as much as possible) has much to do with how I treat fingerings on the higher strings.

These anthologies are dedicated to my graduate guitar professor, William Gangel (1955-2007), who mentioned that he was working on a comparable compendium, but alas, he was taken before its completion. I consider this work as an extension of his idea and am grateful for his teachings and encouragement. It is also dedicated to all the working and concertizing guitarists for whom the content of this oeuvre was designed. Special thanks to Dr. Kevin Mooney for his textual editing and Karla Cruz for her help in making selections, providing scores for reference and textual editing.

Mark Anthony Cruz

About the Author

Mark Cruz is originally from Oklahoma City, Oklahoma. His formal training began when he attended Oklahoma City University in 1984 where he studied guitar with Michael Millard and composition with Frank Payne. In 1989 he entered the first annual national composition contest for solo guitar sponsored by the University of Arizona and placed second with his *Trilogy for Guitar*. After earning his undergraduate degree in guitar performance, he went on to earn a Masters degree at Southwest Texas State University (Now Texas State University). While there, he studied composition with Dr. Russell Riepe and guitar with William Gangel, whom he succeeded as professor of guitar from 1999 to the present.

As a composer, Cruz has been published by Shawnee Press, Soundboard Magazine, Mel Bay Publications, and Clear Note Publications while managing his own company, MAC Publications. He was the first-prize winner of the Austin Classical Guitar sponsored composition competition in 2006, '07, '08, '10 and '17. He has received numerous commissions including: Nevada's Clark County School District for their 2022 Honor Guitar Ensemble, San Antonio SummerFest 2022, Kossler Duo in 2020, Beatty Music Competition in Washington D. C. 2015, Sarah Herbert (a DMA student from the Cincinnati Conservatory, 2016), Brett Floyd (DMA student from the University of South Carolina, 2013), Classical Minds Guitar Festival, Houston, Texas, and University Baptist Church in Austin, TX (for choir and organ for their 100th anniversary celebration). Mr. Cruz's *Triptych* for solo guitar has been performed internationally by guitarist, Adam Holzman. Such notable artists as Austin Guitar Quartet, Presti Trio, TxGQ and the Hanser/McClellan Duo have also performed his work in addition to numerous high schools and universities across the United States and abroad.

As a performer, Cruz placed 1st in the 2022 Indiana Fingerstyle Competition and 1st in the 2013 Winfield International Fingerstyle Competition. He was a featured artist at Dr. Isaac Bustos' Southwest Guitar Symposium in 2022, San Antonio SummerFest 2022 (with his jazz quartet), Dr. Joseph Williams' Texas Guitar Conference in 2016, Dr. Bustos' Houston Classical Guitar Workshop in 2016 and '17, Dr. Michael Quantz's Brownsville Guitar Ensemble Festival in 2014 (as a lecturer), Valerie Hartzell's Classical Minds Guitar Festival in Houston, TX in 2009 and 2014, and Enrique Madriguera's Eastfield Guitar Festival in Dallas, TX in 2008. Cruz also performed Vivaldi concerti with the Oklahoma City Philharmonic and Ballet in 1993 and '98. Five of Cruz's CDs have been featured on the internationally syndicated radio program *Classical Guitar Alive*. Two of his all-original CDs received positive reviews in the scholarly periodical, *Soundboard*.

As a teacher, Cruz's students have won top prizes in the national Brownsville Guitar Ensemble Festival. In the summer of 2015, he taught at the Narnia Music Festival in Narni, Italy. Many of his former students are active in the Texas education system.

Pavan No. 1

Fingering: M. A. Cruz

Luis Milan
(c. 1500 - c. 1561)

6-2-20

Pavan No. 3

Fingering: M. A. Cruz

Luis Milan
(c. 1500 - c. 1561)

6-3-20

Guárdame las Vacas

Fingering: M. A. Cruz

Luis de Narváez
(1490 - 1547)

6-19-20

Alman

Fingering: M. A. Cruz

Robert Johnson
(1583 - 1633)

6-20-20

Come Again

Arr. M. A. Cruz

John Dowland
(1563 - 1626)

5-23-20

Ballo 'plus de tristesse ta maitresse'

Adaptation: M. A. Cruz

Francesco da Milano
(1497 - 1543)

6-18-20

Couplet

(Combined studies from Sixty Short Reading Exercises, Studies and Pieces)

Mark Anthony Cruz
(b. 1963)

Study No. 57

(from Sixty Short Reading Exercises, Studies and Pieces)

Mark Anthony Cruz
(b. 1963)

Affettuoso

(from Sonata for Flute, RV 48)

Arr: M. A. Cruz

Antonio Vivaldi
(1678 - 1741)

2-14-05

Minuetto and Trio

(from Grande Sonata, Op.25)

Fingering: M. A. Cruz

Fernando Sor
(1778 - 1839)

Lascia Ch'io Pianga

(Aria from Rinaldo)

Adaptation: M. A. Cruz

Georg Frederic Handel
(1685 - 1759)

5-20-20

Allegro

(from Concerto in D, RV 93)

Adaptation: M. A. Cruz

Antonio Vivaldi
(1678 - 1741)

9-9-20

Allegro

Adaptation: M. A. Cruz

Joseph Haydn
(1732 - 1809)

7-13-20

Ständchen

Adaptation: M. A. Cruz

Franz Schubert
(1797 - 1828)

Andante Moderato

The Star-Spangled Banner

Arr: M. A. Cruz

John Stafford Smith
(1750 - 1836)

6-26-20

God Save the Queen

(Op. 6, No. 10)

Adaptation: Fernando Sor
Fingering: M. A. Cruz

Anonymous

7-14-20

*possible B flat rather than B natural.

Battle Hymn of the Republic

American Folk Song | **Arr: Mark Anthony Cruz (b. 1963)**

c. 2000
rev. 7-21-20

Excerpt from

Military March No. 1

(from Pomp and Circumstance Military Marches, Op. 39)

Adaptation: M. A. Cruz

Edward Elgar
(1857 - 1934)

7-22-20

Excerpts from

Wedding Day at Tröldhaugen

(Op. 65, No. 6)

Adaptation: M. A. Cruz

Edvard Grieg
(1843 - 1907)

Trumpet Tune

Adaptation: M. A. Cruz

Jeremiah Clarke (1674 - 1707)

5-19-20

Thaxted

(excerpt from Jupiter from The Planets)

Adaptation: M. A. Cruz

Gustav Holst
(1874 - 1934)

6-23-20

The Water Is Wide

Scottish Folk Song

Arr: Mark Anthony Cruz
(b. 1963)

Londonderry Air
(Danny Boy)

Traditional Irish Melody

Arr: Mark Anthony Cruz (b. 1963)

8-5-20

Sheep May Safely Graze
(from Cantata BWV 208)

Adaptation: M. A. Cruz

Johann Sebastian Bach
(1685 - 1750)

5-30-20

Excerpts from

Sleepers, Wake

(from Cantata No. 140, BWV 645)

Adaptation: M. A. Cruz

Johann Sebastian Bach
(1685 - 1750)

*jump to m. 32 for an abridged version

(*)
6-9-20

Andante

(from Concerto for Two Mandolins, RV 532)

Adaptation: M. A. Cruz

Antonio Vivaldi
(1678 - 1741)

hVII
VII
hVII hV hIII
simili
5-18-20

Hornpipe

(No. 13 from Water Musik HWV 349)

Adaptation: M. A. Cruz

Georg Frederic Handel
(1685 - 1759)

Fine
D.C. al Fine
5-26-20

The Arrival of the Queen of Sheba

Adaptation: M. A. Cruz

Georg Frederic Handel
(1685 - 1759)

pont.
nat.
cresc.

cresc.
6-10-20

In the Hall of the Mountain King

(from Peer Gynt - Suite No. 1 Op. 46)

Adaptation: M. A. Cruz

Edvard Grieg
(1843 - 1907)

II
VII
hVII
VIII
IX
hIV
V
p
9-5-20

Anitra's Dance

(from Peer Gynt - Suite No. 1 Op. 46)

Adaptation: M. A. Cruz

Edvard Grieg
(1843 - 1907)

6-12-20

Polovtsian Dance

(from Prince Igor)

Adaptation: M. A. Cruz

Alexander Borodin
(1833 - 1887)

5-20-20

Excerpts from

Sicilienne

(Op. 78)

Adaptation: M. A. Cruz

Gabriel Fauré
(1845 - 1924)

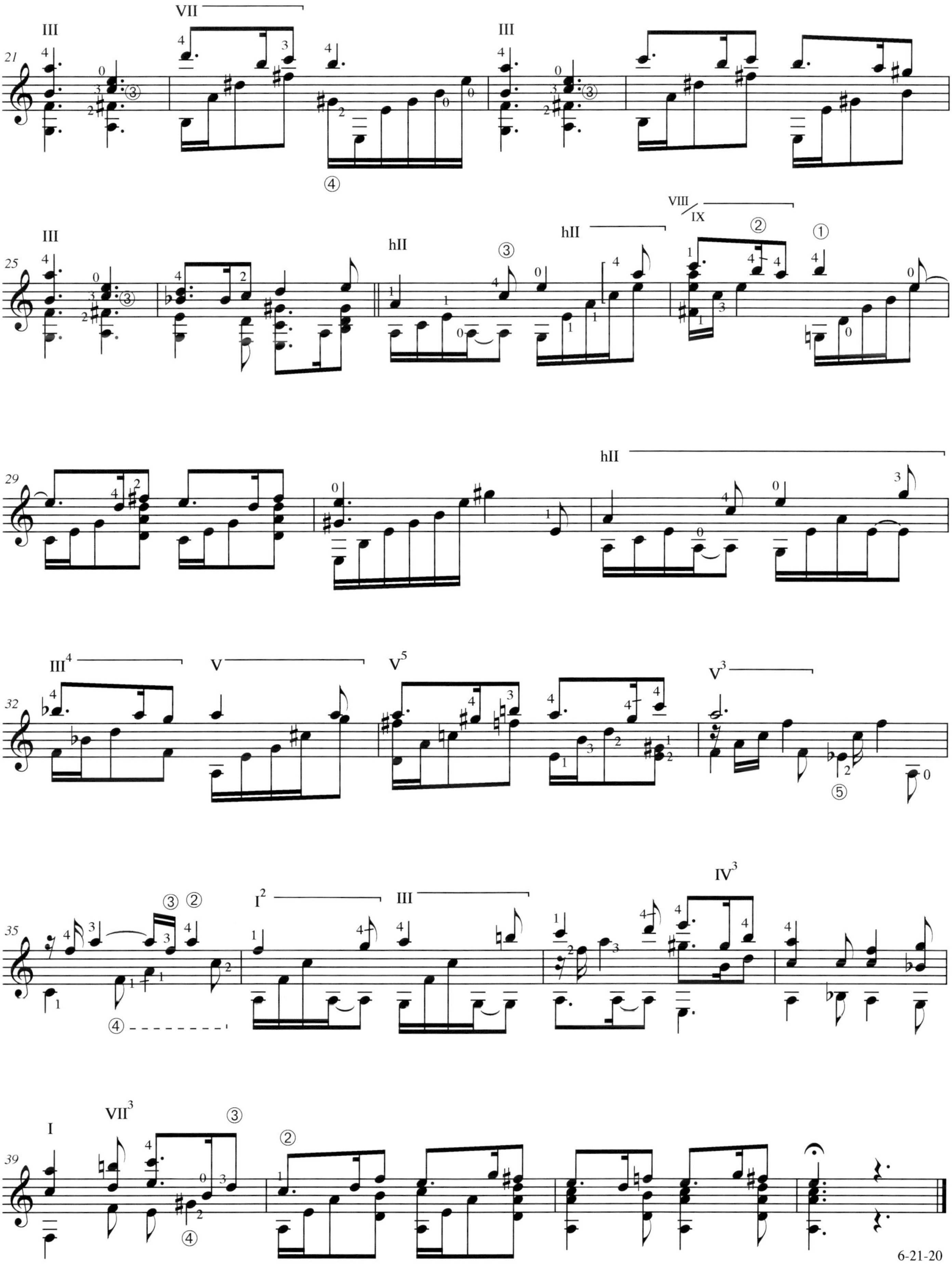
III
VII
hII
VIII/IX
III4
V
V5
V3
I2
IV3
I
VII3
6-21-20

From Prelude and Fugue in d Minor. Originally composed for two guitars.
Commissioned by the Kossler Duo

Kossler Prelude

Mark Anthony Cruz
(b. 1963)

contemplative
rit.
nat. harm.
4-27-20

Für Elise

Adaptation: M. A. Cruz

Ludwig van Beethoven
(1770 - 1827)

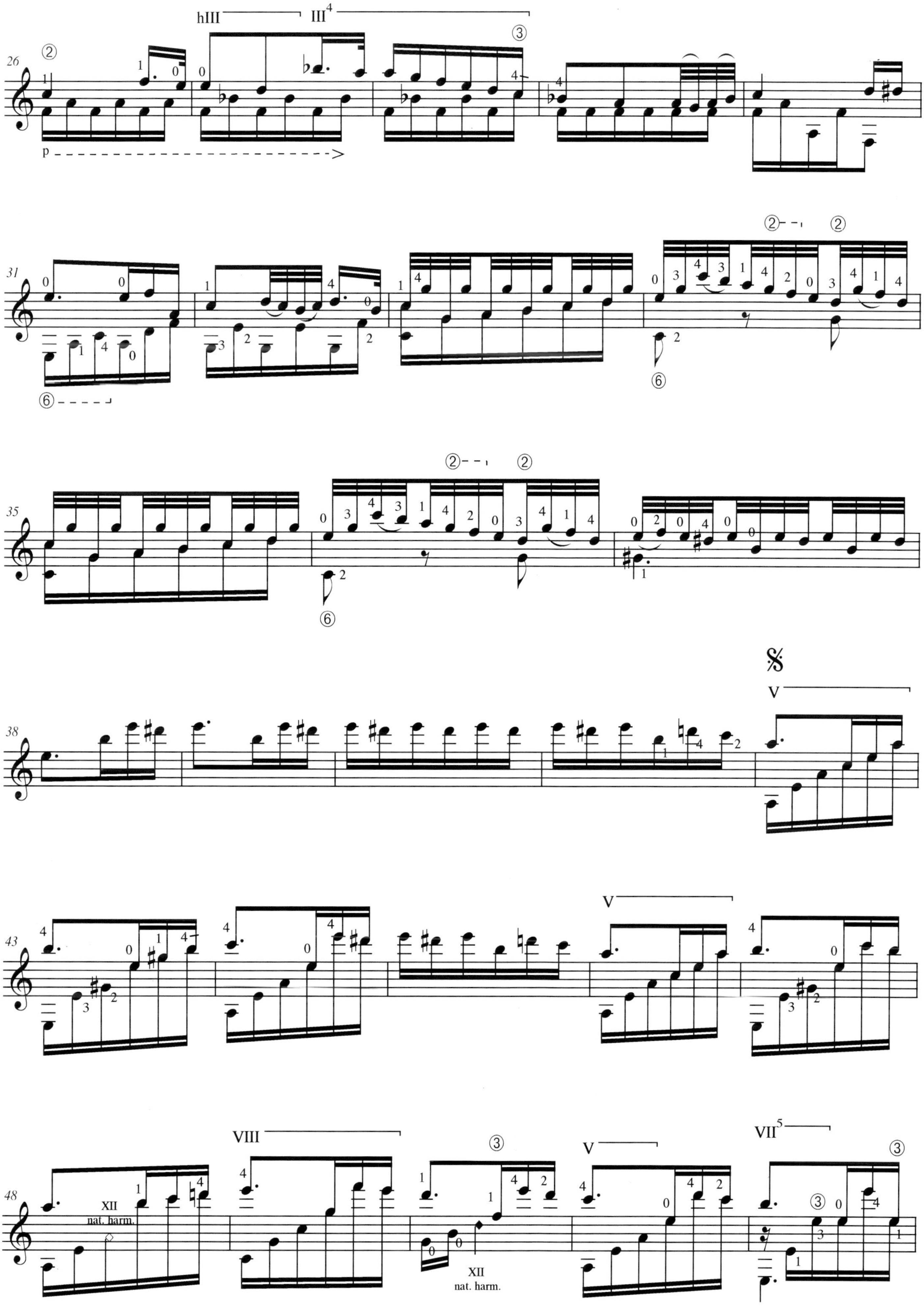
hIII
III
p
V
VIII
XII
nat. harm.
VII

5-17-20

Cello Suite No. 1

(BWV 1007)

Adaptation: M. A. Cruz

Prelude

Johann Sebastian Bach
(1685 - 1750)

II5
p i m i m i
p i m a m i
p i m p m i
p i a i a i
II3
p i a i a i m
V
i m a m i m i p
II3

Allemande

XII
nat. harm.

Courante

(or play in 1st position)

Sarabande

Menuet I

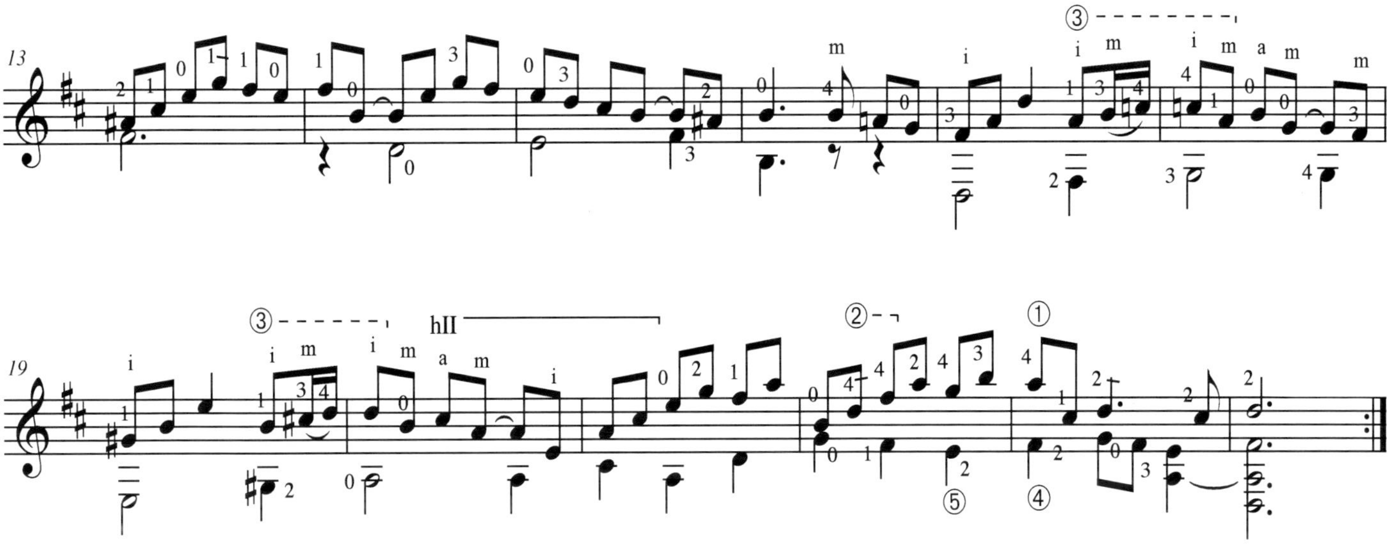

Menuet II

Gigue

4-20-20

Sonata K. 334

Adaptation: M. A. Cruz | **Domenico Scarlatti (1685 - 1757)**

hII
hIV IV5
hIV IV5
VII
IV5
VI
VII
IX

4-4-20

Prelude

(BWV 999)

Trans. M. A. Cruz

Johann Sebastian Bach
(1685 - 1750)

22
IX5
VIII3
25
V3
II5
28
31
34
II4
VII3
37
hV
40
I3
5-1-20

Fugue
(BWV 1000)

Fingering. M. A. Cruz

Johann Sebastian Bach
(1685 - 1750)

m i p p m i
hII
5-17-20

Maria

Gavotte

Fingering: M. A. Cruz

Francisco Tárrega
(1852 - 1909)

VII
nat. harm.
XII
nat. harm.
pizz.
6-16-20

Malagueña Fácil

Fingering: M. A. Cruz

Francisco Tárrega
(1852 - 1909)

* Optional skip to 1st measure of Cruz Malagueña for a seamless pairing.

Malagueña

Mark Anthony Cruz
(b. 1963)

* small arrows indicate literal direction of strumming.

7-30-20

Overture

Fingering: M. A. Cruz

Fernando Carulli
(1770 - 1841)

hII

D.S. al Coda
9th position

6-7-20

Vals

(Op. 8, No. 4)

Fingering: M. A. Cruz

Águstin Barrios Mangoré
(1885 - 1944)

Trio Lento
espress.
port.
D. C. al Coda
no repeats
campanella →
p i a m p i
moviendo poco a poco

*supporting chord optional

7-16-20

Julia Florida

Fingering: M. A. Cruz

Águstin Barrios Mangoré
(1885 - 1944)

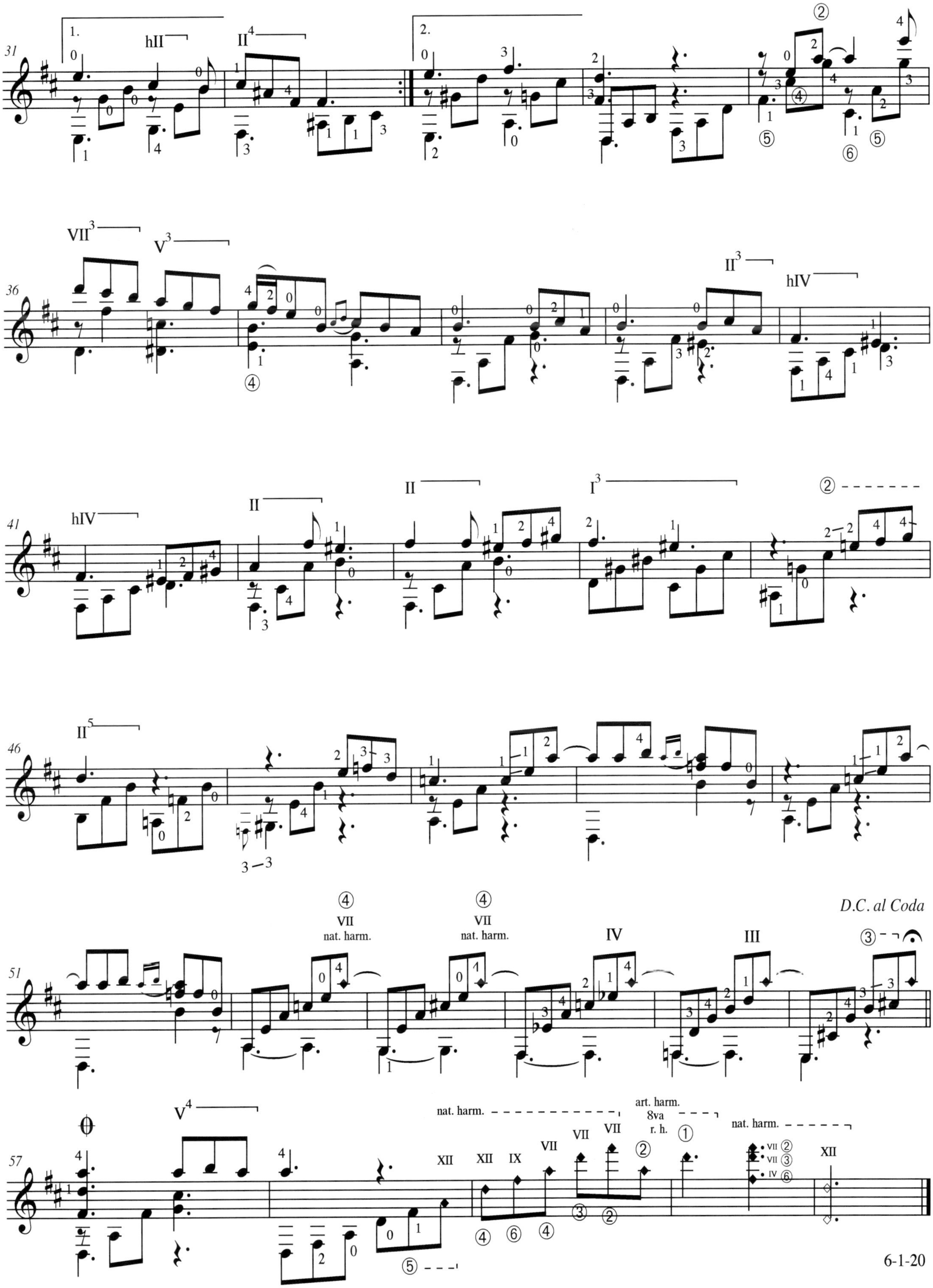
D.C. al Coda
nat. harm.
art. harm.
8va
r. h.
6-1-20

O Sacred Head Now Wounded

(Matthew Passion)

Arr: M. A. Cruz

Johann Sebastian Bach
(1685 - 1750)

3-3-21

Divertimento

I. Rondo

Mark Anthony Cruz
(b. 1963)

1.
2.
III
II
rit.

II. Sonata

III. Air

IV. Capricho

VII
VII
III
IX
VIII
VII
rit.
a tempo
i m i m i

7-11-06
rev. 7-19

Theme and Variations on

God Rest Ye, Merry Gentlemen

English Tune

Mark Anthony Cruz
(b. 1963)

II
1.
2.
V
nat. harm.
5th position

c. 11-92
revised c. 12 -14

Angels We Have Heard on High

Traditional French

Mark Anthony Cruz
(b. 1963)

1st page: 7-19-20
2nd page: 12-22-91

Coventry Carol

English 14th Century

Mark Anthony Cruz
(b. 1963)

nat. harm.
V
9th position
nat. harm.
XII
nat. harm.
XII
2.
nat. harm.
XII
nat. harm.
XII

c. 2012
rev. 7-21-20

Excerpts from

March of the Toys

(from Babes in Toyland)

Adaptation: M. A. Cruz

Victor August Herbert
(1859 - 1924)

a tempo
rit.

rit.
III
VIII
I
hVIII
D.S. al Coda
rit.
broad
maestoso
a tempo
hI
c. 9-15

Amazing Grace

Anonymous
Mark Anthony Cruz
(b. 1963)

IX
II
VI4
hVII
IX
VIII
VII
IX2
IX
V4
I
II4
hII
7-30-20

All Creatures of Our God and King

Anonymous
Mark Anthony Cruz
(b. 1963)

majestic
a tempo
molto rit.
8-1-20

Rondo

(Op. 2, No. 3)

Fingering: M. A. Cruz

Dionisio Aguado
(1784 - 1849)

gliss.
gliss.

* Julian Bream skips to measure 170 in his recording.

originally an arpeggio
from D up to A

7-14-20

Christ The Lord Has Risen Today

Anonymous
Mark Anthony Cruz
(b. 1963)

VIII
XII
nat. harm.
VII
n. h.
quicker tempo a la jig
rit.
rit.
a tempo
rall.

a tempo
molto rit.
XII
nat. harm.
c. 1999
rev. 4-7-20